To the Reader...

   Our purpose in creating this series is to provide young readers with accurate accounts of the lives of Native American men and women important in the history of their tribes. The stories are written by scholars, including American Indians.

   Native Americans are as much a part of North American life today as they were one hundred years ago. Even in times past, Indians were not all the same. Not all of them lived in teepees or wore feather warbonnets. They were not all warriors. Some did fight against the white man, but many befriended him.

   Whether patriot or politician, athlete or artist, Arapaho or Zuni, the story of each person in this series deserves to be told. Whether the individuals gained distinction on the battlefield or the playing field, in the courtroom or the classroom, they have enriched the heritage and history of all Americans. It is hoped that those who read their stories will realize that many different peoples, regardless of culture or color, have played a part in shaping the United States and Canada, in making both countries what they are today.

Herman J. Viola
General Editor
Author of *Exploring the West*
and other volumes on the West
and Native Americans

GENERAL EDITOR
Herman J. Viola
Author of *Exploring the West* and other volumes on the West
and Native Americans

MANAGING EDITOR
Robert M. Kvasnicka
Coeditor of *The Commissioners of Indian Affairs, 1824-1977*
Coeditor of *Indian-White Relations: A Persistent Paradox*

MANUSCRIPT EDITOR
Eric Newman

PROJECT MANAGER
Joyce Spicer

PRODUCTION
Jack Reichard
Scott Melcer

Published by Steck-Vaughn 1993

Copyright © 1993 Pinnacle Press, Inc., doing business as Rivilo Books

Printed and bound in the United States.

2 3 4 5 6 7 8 9 0   WO   98 97 96 95 94

Library of Congress Cataloging-in-Publication Data
Erdrich, Heidi Ellen.
   Maria Tallchief / text by Heidi Ellen Erdrich; illustrations by
Rick Whipple.
        p.   cm. — (American Indian stories)
   "A Rivilo book."
   Summary: Describes the life of the American ballerina and
descendant of the Osage tribe.
   ISBN 0-8114-6577-2   —   ISBN 0-8114-4099-0 (soft cover)
   1. Tallchief, Maria — Juvenile literature.   2. Dancers —
United States — Biography — Juvenile literature.   3. Osage
Indians — Biography — Juvenile literature.   [1. Tallchief, Maria.
2. Dancers.   3. Osage Indians — Biography.   4. Indians of North
America — Biography.]   I. Whipple, Rick, ill.   II. Title.
III. Series.
GV1785.T32E73   1993
792.8'028'092 — dc20
[B]   92-12256
                                                   CIP AC

MARIA
TALLCHIEF

Text by Heidi Ellen Erdrich
Illustrations by Rick Whipple

A RIVILO BOOK

RSVP
RAINTREE
STECK-VAUGHN
PUBLISHERS
The Steck-Vaughn Company
Austin, Texas

The great American ballerina Maria Tallchief came from the American Indian tribe called the Osage. An old Osage story says that the people of the stars in the sky came down and met the people of the earth. The two kinds of people became one. They were called "The People of the Middle Waters," another name for the Osage.

Maria also came from two kinds of people. Her mother, Ruth Mary Porter, was white. Her father, Alexander Tall Chief, was a full-blood Osage.

Maria was born in 1925 in Fairfax, Oklahoma. Her birth name was Elizabeth Marie Tall Chief. Her family called her Betty Marie. She had a younger sister, Marjorie, who also grew up to be a famous dancer. They were members of two important Osage families, the Big Hearts and the Tall Chiefs. Many tribal leaders had come from those families.

5

When the white people came, the Osage were living in
villages located along the Little Osage River in what is now
western Missouri. Several families shared one long house,
or lodge. These lodges were made from a hickory-tree
framework covered with tree bark and mats. The women
made the mats from the stems of cattail plants that they
collected from marshy areas. Some families lived in tepees,
which were cone-shaped tents. Tepees had a frame of
wooden poles. The frame was covered with animal hides.

The Osage were farmers and hunters. They planted corn, beans, and squash for food. They also grew gourds that they used for containers and musical instruments. The forest provided wild berries and nuts to eat. It also provided plants for medicines to cure the sick. When meat was needed, the Osage men hunted with bows and arrows. They started using guns to hunt after the white people came. When an Indian killed a bison, no part of the animal was wasted. The meat fed many people. The bison hides were used to make blankets, robes, and other clothing. Bison ribs were even used to make sleds for Osage children to use in the snow.

In 1808 the United States government began buying land from the Osage. The government moved them to an area that is now the state of Oklahoma.

Their new home was called the Osage Reservation. The land was not good for farming, but oil was found there in 1896. Suddenly, the Osage were very rich. The tribal leaders were wise in the way they managed the oil money. The Osage shared the money with one another so that no one in the tribe had to be poor.

Over the years, the Osage came to live like the white people. When they became wealthy, some Osage bought fancy cars and moved into big houses. Their lives were much like those of rich white people. Sometimes, however, an old tepee or a long house stood in the backyard of a fine house.

Maria's family lived in a brick house. Only English was spoken in Maria's home. Their Indian grandmother, Eliza Big Heart Tall Chief, lived in the house, too. She made certain that Maria and Marjorie learned about the Osage and the way they lived before the whites came. She told them old tribal stories of magical spirit birds who spoke to the Osage.

Grandma Eliza took the little girls to Osage dances. The Osage loved to dance. Before they learned about the white people's religion, they danced to honor their great spirit Wah'Kon-Tah, the giver of life. They also danced to celebrate important events in their lives. Because the dances reminded the Osage of the time before the whites came, the government thought dancing made the Indians difficult to control. The dances were outlawed for a time, but now they are performed on special occasions.

At the dances, Maria saw men and women dressed in colorful costumes made from beads, feathers, and animal skins. She heard the high "falsetto" singing and the beat of the drum. The drumbeats and the dance steps sounded like heartbeats. After she got home from the dances, Maria tried to make Osage music on the family piano.

Maria had a great talent for all musical things. Her mother wanted her to be a concert pianist, so Maria took piano lessons. Maria liked playing the piano, but she also was interested in dancing. A dance teacher came to the Tall Chiefs' home to give the girls ballet lessons. Maria and Marjorie dressed up in black tights and pink ballet slippers for their lessons. They looked like twins with their black hair, dark eyes, and oval faces. Their teacher taught them how to dance "on points" — that is, on their toes. Soon they were whirling around the room, dancing on the tips of their toes.

Grandma Eliza was glad that the girls liked to dance. Even though they were not learning Osage dances, she knew that any kind of dancing would make their bodies strong.

When Maria was about eight years old, her family moved to Los Angeles, California. Her parents thought that the music and dance teachers would be better there. At first, the children at Maria's new school made fake "Indian war whoops" and teased her about her American Indian last name. Maria didn't let the teasing bother her. She was happy because she had a new dance teacher.

Maria and Marjorie went to Ernest Belcher's dance studio. There they learned acrobatics, tap, and Spanish and ballet dancing. On the first day, Maria and Marjorie jumped about and twirled on tiptoe. The teacher was very upset. He said that the girls' feet were too small for dancing on their toes. They could have been injured for life. He made the girls promise not to dance on their toes until they were older. They worked very hard practicing other dance steps every day. Maria also spent a great deal of time practicing piano. With school, piano, and dance, Maria was a very busy little girl.

Finally, the girls got the chance to dance for an audience. Because they were Osage, the teacher had them do what was supposed to be an "Indian" dance. It was nothing like the real Osage dances Maria had seen. There were no gourd rattles or eagle-bone whistles to make the music. The girls did not sway slowly with pride like the Osage women. Instead, they jumped around like wild things. Still, it was better than not dancing on stage at all.

Maria was twelve before she got to wear a tutu, a ballet dancer's short dress. She wore it to perform in a recital. The tutu was made of yellow net and was very soft. Maria floated across the stage in her lovely dress as free as a butterfly. This recital was special for another reason. In it, Maria was able to reveal both her talents. She danced for half of the program and played the piano for the other half.

Although she continued to study piano, Maria thought more and more about ballet. When she was about fifteen, she had a chance to study with one of the greatest ballet teachers, Bronislava Nijinska. Maria called her Madame. Madame was the sister of the great Russian ballet dancer Vaslav Nijinsky.

Maria worked harder than ever for the teacher she liked so well. Her dancing became so good that she was asked to perform in a special show of Madame's.

Under a star-filled sky, many people watched Maria dance at the Hollywood Bowl, a large outdoor theater. She was performing in the *Chopin Concerto*, a ballet created by Madame.

As the music flowed, Maria moved gracefully across the stage. Then, suddenly, she slipped! It was the worst thing a dancer could do. Maria kept on dancing and tried not to cry. As soon as she finished, Madame comforted her. Madame reminded Maria that her slip was not the end of the world.

Maria continued to dance. Playing the piano was important. Dancing, however, was something she absolutely needed. Maria decided that she really wanted to be a professional dancer and not a pianist.

After Maria graduated from Beverly Hills High School, she went to New York City. She quickly got a lucky break. A man who had seen her perform in Los Angeles was looking for dancers to join the ballet company known as the Ballet Russe de Monte Carlo, for a tour of Canada. He hired Maria for the "corps de ballet," a large group of dancers. In this group, young girls can gain the experience necessary to become outstanding dancers.

In Canada, Maria's life was very exciting. She studied many small parts, dancing them over and over to make them perfect. Maria learned the dances so that she would be able to perform them in case something happened to the star ballerina. Maria knew that she was ready to perform the leading role. It seemed to her, however, that she would never get a chance to do it.

Finally, the time came when she was needed for the lead. Maria danced so well that everyone said she was going to be a great ballerina. She began to get better parts to dance. The Ballet Russe then asked her to stay with the group permanently.

All her life Maria had been called Betty Marie Tall Chief. The people who ran the Ballet Russe wanted her name to sound more like those of the great European ballet dancers. She agreed to change her first name to Maria. She was proud of her Osage last name, and she would not change it. Instead, she made it one word: Tallchief.

It was thrilling for an American Indian to dance ballet as well as the Europeans did. Newspaper writers called Maria "The Beautiful Dancing Osage Princess." Maria thought this was strange because the Osage did not have princesses.

In May 1943, Maria danced the *Chopin Concerto* again. This was the dance that Maria had slipped in years before. This time, however, she danced it perfectly. At last, she had shown everyone her best. After the performance, the audience cheered loudly. The other young dancers gave Maria an armful of red roses.

Then George Balanchine came to work with the Ballet Russe. Balanchine was famous as a teacher and as a choreographer, the person who arranges the dances. He made Maria work harder than ever. She enjoyed working for Balanchine. She danced with more grace and feeling whenever he was nearby.

Balanchine trained Maria to dance the part of a fairy in a ballet called *The Fairy's Kiss*. Maria danced the role so well that people cheered enthusiastically. Maria had proven that she was as good as the European dancers.

In New York City, Maria's sister, Marjorie, was becoming successful as a ballet dancer, as well. Other American Indian ballet dancers at the time were Roselle Hightower, a Choctaw Indian, and Yvonne Chouteau, a Cherokee.

Yvonne Chouteau

Marjorie Tallchief

Maria Tallchief

Rosella Hightower

23

In 1946 Maria and George Balanchine were married. They left the Ballet Russe in 1947 to spend a season with the Paris Opera Company. Maria's fans threw flowers on stage at the end of her dances and sent her gifts. People said that Maria made magic when she danced. Balanchine helped her dance even better by creating dances for her that showed off her special abilities.

When Maria and Balanchine returned to the United States, they worked with the Ballet Society. This organization eventually became the New York City Ballet Company. Maria was the company's prima, or first, ballerina.

In 1949 Balanchine asked Maria to dance the starring role in *The Firebird*, the story of a magical creature, half bird and half woman. It was a difficult part to dance, but Maria remembered the stories her grandmother had told her about a time when spirit birds spoke to the Osage. Maria tried to capture the feeling of this magic in her performance.

Dressed in the colors of a flame, Maria leapt across the stage. Her red and orange feathered dress glowed as she soared and spun. Gold dust on her arms and shoulders shimmered like fire. To those who watched her, it was as if she really were a firebird. They knew they were seeing one of the greatest dancers of all time.

Maria went on to dance two of the most famous parts in the world of ballet. In *Swan Lake*, she played the Queen of the Swans. In *The Nutcracker*, Maria had one of the most difficult parts a ballerina can dance — the Sugar Plum Fairy. In these roles and many others, she proved to be worthy of being known all over the world as the first Native American prima ballerina.

Another great honor was given to Maria by her own tribe. The Osage staged a great celebration for her in Fairfax in 1953. The tribe danced, made speeches, and sang Osage songs. They had a feast of Indian foods such as corn soup and fry bread. Maria dressed in Osage clothes. She wore a crown decorated with beads that formed beautiful designs.

The Osage had always been a proud, dignified, and courageous people. They gave Maria an honor name. This was a name her tribe would call her because she made them proud. Her grandmother selected the name *Wa-Xthe-Thonba*, which means Woman of Two Standards or of Two Worlds. This name showed that Maria belonged to both the Osage and the white worlds. Maria had been cheered many times before. The best time, however, was when the Osage cheered and clapped for Woman of Two Worlds.

True to her new name, Maria did not forget the American Indian world while she danced in the white world. In 1957 she performed with an Iroquois man named Tom Two Arrows. Wearing a tribal costume and a headdress made from porcupine quills, he performed dances from his tribe. Wearing a pink satin tutu and a jeweled crown, Maria danced ballet. Together Maria and Tom showed that American Indians could keep the old ways alive and still be part of the larger world.

In 1960 Maria joined the American Ballet Theatre as its prima ballerina. Eventually she returned to the New York City Ballet. In 1966 Maria decided to hang up her ballet slippers and retire. She had toured and danced all over the world with great success. Now, she felt she should spend time at home with her family. Her marriage to Balanchine had not lasted. Her second husband was Henry D. Paschen, Jr. They had a daughter, Elise Maria.

In 1967 an Indian organization called the Council of Fire awarded Maria the Indian Achievement Award. She also was made a member of the council. Maria spoke to American Indian groups about Indians and the arts. She also took part in programs at various universities to educate students about Native Americans. Maria continued her association with the dance world as well. For several years, she was the artistic director for the Lyric Opera Ballet in Chicago. In 1980 Maria and Marjorie founded the Chicago City Ballet. Marjorie, too, had enjoyed great success. Her career, however, had been centered largely in Europe. She danced with the de Cuevas Company and with the Paris Opera Ballet.

Betty Marie, Wa-Xthe-Thonba, Woman of Two Worlds, Prima Ballerina — these names all belong to a woman known around the world as one of the greatest dancers ever: Maria Tallchief.

Marjorie

Maria

HISTORY OF MARIA TALLCHIEF

1925	Maria Tallchief was born Elizabeth Marie Tall Chief on January 24, in Fairfax, Oklahoma.
1934	Maria's family moved to Los Angeles, California.
1942	Maria graduated from Beverly Hills High School and joined the Ballet Russe de Monte Carlo.
1943	Maria danced her first major part with the Ballet Russe.
1946	Maria married George Balanchine.
1947	Maria and Balanchine left the Ballet Russe. They joined the Ballet Society, which later became the New York City Ballet. Maria became its leading dancer.
1949	Maria enjoyed great success in *The Firebird*.
1952	Maria danced *Swan Lake*. Her marriage to Balanchine ended.
1953	Oklahoma declared June 29 Maria Tallchief Day.
1955	Maria toured Europe.
1956	Maria married Henry D. Paschen, Jr.
1959	Maria's daughter, Elise Maria, was born.
1960	Maria toured the Soviet Union and joined the American Ballet Theatre.
1966	Maria retired to spend time with her family.
1967	Maria received the Indian Achievement Award.
1980	Maria and her sister, Marjorie Tallchief, established the Chicago City Ballet.